It Takes Courage

*A Monologue,
Readers' Theaters,
And Scripts
For Drama Ministry*

Pam Speights

CSS Publishing Company, Inc., Lima, Ohio

IT TAKES COURAGE

For more information about CSS Publishing Company resources, visit our website at www.csspub.com or email us at custserv@csspub.com or call (800) 241-4056.

Cover design by Barbara Spencer with Logan Speights
ISBN: 978-0-7880-2444-3
ISBN-10: 0-7880-2444-2

PRINTED IN U.S.A.

*To those who use their talents
to serve the Lord in creative ways*

May he bless your efforts

Table Of Contents

Introduction

Finding good material is the first challenge of all theater directors. It drives all other decisions. Especially scarce in the Christian arena are scripts that touch hearts and at the same time, develop the actor's craft. A middle-school teacher struggles to find material with age-appropriate, engaging content. A youth group would love acting opportunities that communicate in a way that is meaningful and creative. A church drama director seeks material that is easy to orchestrate, with messages that touch the hearts of mixed-age audiences. A script that enables the director to use minimal staging and still present a powerful message is a treasure.

I have been there. As a drama coordinator at church and as a teacher at a Christian high school for many years, I was in constant search of material. I needed scripts suitable for youth and adult casts, but it was (and still is) difficult to find any religious or morally themed scripts, so I began writing. The scripts, monologues, and readers' theater selections shared in this book are award winning. I wrote them and subsequently performed them in contest settings, receiving top honors. Additionally, they have been well received in devotional settings with audiences from ten to 500 in attendance. While your purpose may not be to win a contest, it is always nice to know that the material you are using has been affirmed by others.

In the end, it's all in the message. Theater entertains while revealing truths about our existence. And the message found within these pages is one to be applauded. God is ever present, worthy of honor, and has placed challenges in our lives to help us grow.

The challenge is before you. May you be blessed in it.

Synopses

Be A Blessing

This original drama features a flexible teen cast of five actors — the gender is not important. It is based on the true story of a preacher who challenged his congregation.

What's In Your Backpack?

This sketch features a cast of teens, two female and one male, plus flexible roles for four to eight additional actors. Set during an in-school suspension, this sketch is about trusting God and finding blessings in the midst of trials.

Where Is Courage?

This action drama features a cast of five young people, both male and female, working as an ensemble. It portrays a child's journey in the search for true bravery.

Every Knee Shall Bow

This is a readers' theater featuring four adult voices and also includes singing. It was inspired by the writings of Robert Beasley and is based on Revelation, chapters 5 and 6.

The Joy We Share

This readers' theater sketch features four female voices. It is based on Psalm 28:7, "The Lord is my strength and my shield; my heart trusts in him, and I am helped."

Who Is In Control?

This is a monologue featuring one adult female portraying the mother of the apostle Paul. An optional narrator voice may introduce the character.

Be A Blessing
The Preacher's Challenge

Theme

This sketch is based on the true story of a preacher and the challenge he gave his congregation.

Cast

Flexible cast of five

Staging

In this style of theater, each performer is both a narrator and a player on the stage. The cast is dressed similarly, creating an ensemble effect. No props are needed, no sets are needed, making it very mobile. All cast members are on stage throughout the sketch.

During the introduction, the players stand still, facing the audience.

```
   A                          B
        C            D
            E
   ━━━━━━━━━━━━━━━━━━
```

E: We, as the church, are called to be a blessing to the world.

C: We know there is joy in being a Christian.

All: Some do not.

D: We know that there is comfort and peace and security even in the middle of tragedy.

All: Some do not.

A: We know about a Savior.

All: Some do not.

B: So how do we get the good news to people?

C: How do you become a blessing?

(Cast breaks and moves forward to sit at E's [preacher] feet, facing him.)

E: Today I have a surprise and a challenge for you. You are all accustomed to giving money at church. Today we are giving money to you. You will each be given an envelope. In your envelope you will find either $2, $5, or $10. Here's your challenge. With the money you are given, you must find a way to be a blessing to someone around you. Go and be lights to the world.

(E pantomimes handing each cast member an envelope. As each stands, they turn and say their line to the audience.)

A: Each person in the congregation received an envelope. Adults and children.

B: In the envelope was money and a small business card.

C: The card said, "This is a blessing from a Christian to you."

D: What can I do with only $2?

(Cast begins to interact with each other.)

A: I don't know. I can't even think of what to do with $10.

B: Well, we won't cure cancer, or feed the world.

C: No, but maybe we can do small acts of kindness that will bring someone to Jesus.

E: And so the challenge began. *(moves upstage and watches the action)*

(Note: Every action does not need to be pantomimed. Two, sometimes three, lines can be spoken while the cast gets into a position to pantomime the next one.)

D: *(says as other cast members pantomime the action)* One young child urged his mom to stop the car and let him give his money to the homeless man under the bridge.

A: *(says as other cast members pantomime the action)* Another knew a friend at school that never had any lunch money.

E: What you do for the least of these, you do also to me.

B: *(says as other cast members pantomime the action)* Another purchased a cake mix and made a cake for a new family in the neighborhood.

C: *(says as other cast members pantomime the action)* A couple of people pooled their money and bought a sweater for someone who needed it.

D: One child heard that a family was saving money to adopt a child from Rhodesia. She gave her $5 to them.

A: One young man bought trash bags and cleaned up a neighborhood park.

B: *(says as other cast members pantomime the action)* Someone spent the money on pencils. At school for several days, each time someone needed a pencil, she gave one away.

E: A cup of cold water in *my* name will not go unrewarded.

C: Several pooled their money and purchased groceries for a family in need.

D: Someone bought a basketball and played ball with a lonely child.

E: Someone exchanged the dollar bills for quarters and went to the hospital. There she gave the quarters to families of the ill so that they could buy coffee from the vending machines.

A: A family combined their money and paid for a young couple with a baby to have a night out while they babysat.

All: *(singing)* Make me a servant, Lord, make me like you. For you were a servant, make me one, too. Make me a servant, do what you must do, to make me a servant, make me like you.

B: *(says to the audience as they return to their original V staging positions)* I learned something from this. I thought I needed to be an adult with lots of Bible knowledge to talk to someone about Christianity.

D: I thought I had to invite people to church to teach them about God.

C: Now I see that I can show Jesus to one person by being kind.

E: By being a blessing.

What's In Your Backpack?
How Could In-School Suspension Be A Good Thing?

Theme

    This is a sketch about trusting God and finding blessings in the midst of trials.

Cast

    Jennifer — falsely accused of drug possession

    Matt — the young man seen "planting" the drugs (nonspeaking)

    Nicole — countercultural-looking teen Jennifer meets in "In-School Suspension"

    Accusers and Police — six persons, male or female, double roles

    Cloud of Witnesses — seven persons, male or female (abbreviated CW)

Props

    Backpack filled with books

    Baggie

    Chairs

Police 1: In an attempt to curb the drug problem in our schools, a "Crime Watchers" policy has been initiated. Anyone turning in a fellow student for drug possession can remain anonymous and, when confirmed, will receive a $500 reward.

(Jennifer enters, carrying a backpack, and is jostled as she makes her way through the crowd of students. All freeze. The audience watches Matt put a baggie into Jennifer's backpack without her knowing it. Grinning, he hurries away. Cast unfreezes. The group changes into three separate groups — The Cloud of Witnesses, the

Police, and the Accusers. Matt crosses to the police and, in panto-mime, we see him inform them that Jennifer has drugs in her back-pack. The Police approach Jennifer and ask her to come with them. Jennifer looks confused. The Cloud of Witnesses comes forward. Jennifer crosses left.)

CW All: You are surrounded by a cloud of witnesses to your faith.

Jennifer: Lord? They don't believe me! I don't know how that stuff got into my backpack. You know the truth. Help me!

CW All: Stand firm, Jennifer. Be still and know.

Jennifer: Rescue me!

CW All: Remember Joseph? He was falsely accused by his employer and thrown into prison for years. God did not rescue him.

CW 2: But what they meant for evil, God used for good.

CW 3: Remember Peter?

CW 4: Remember Paul?

CW 5: Remember the apostles who were falsely accused and thrown into prison and tortured?

CW 6: Remember Christ? He was innocent and he went to his death.

CW 7: Without trials, faith cannot grow.

Accuser 1: Jennifer is a dopehead.

CW All: *(whisper)* Stand firm.

Accuser 2: Jennifer got caught.

CW All: *(whisper)* Stand firm.

Accuser 3: We knew she was bad news.

CW All: *(whisper)* Stand firm.

Accuser 4: She's a liar.

Accuser 5: Admit it!

CW All: *(whisper louder)* Stand firm.

Accuser 6: It's true.

Jennifer: Lord? I can't believe you are letting this happen to me! People are going to think I'm a hypocrite. They know I claim to be a Christian and now they all think I'm a fake. Why would you want this to happen?

CW All: Stand firm, Jennifer. God loves you.

Police 1: After reviewing the surveillance tape, we know you are innocent. We saw a young man put the bag into your backpack.

Jennifer: Oh, I'm so glad this is over!

Police 1: No, I'm sorry. The policy is that you were caught with the drugs, and even though we know you are innocent, you must go to In-School Suspension.

Jennifer: You are joking. That is *not* fair.

(Police lead Jennifer off and the ensemble changes to the Cloud of Witnesses surrounding Jennifer and another student, Nicole.)

Nicole: *(sarcastically)* Welcome to ISS, In-School Suspension, also called the "island of misfit toys." The place where those who don't fit in mainstream Happyville live.

(Jennifer sits down quietly and starts pulling books out of her bag.)

Nicole: Try hard not to make eye contact with any of us deviants. Someone might see you, and there goes your nomination for prom queen!

Jennifer: *(after a long look, pauses, then bursts into good-natured laughing, completely shocking Nicole)* That's funny! And if I'm on the island of misfit toys, then I'm definitely where I belong.

Nicole: You? *(pauses and backs off the sarcasm)* Don't think so. We all know that we deserve being here. You don't. I was just messing with you. So, are you planning your revenge? I'll bet you would like to strangle Matt.

Jennifer: Nah.

Nicole: No? Why not?

Jennifer: Well, I learned so much today, he actually did me a favor. I learned who my real friends are, I'm making a new friend, and I didn't have to take Mr. Smith's chemistry test! God is *good!*

Where Is Courage?
A Child's Journey

Theme

This sketch features a child's search for true bravery.

Cast

Group ensemble with five players, all portraying children. They should be dressed alike.

Staging

The action is played out as the lines are spoken, and the characters "build" the set pieces. For instance, when the action calls for a bicycle, the members of the cast "become" a bicycle. Someone becomes the seat, someone else the handlebars, others are the wheels.

———

(Cast, locked arm-in-arm, skip in place.)

Player 1: Five friends went out to play, *(all skip)*

Player 2: not to search for buried treasure, *(all skip)*

All: Nah ...

Player 3: not to chase butterflies, *(all skip)*

All: Nah ...

Player 4: but to find courage.

All: Courage? *(drop action and sit on floor)*

Player 5: How do you find courage?

Player 1: What does courage look like?

Player 2: What does courage sound like?

Player 3: *(jumps up)* Let's go find it.

(others begin to rise)

Player 4: I think I know where to find it!

Player 5: You do?

(group begins forming bicycle)

Player 4: Sure! When you get on the bike, away you go,

(Group forms a bicycle with one rider. As they begin to move, all fall down — complete with childish sound effects.)

Player 1: but you fall and never want to try again.

Player 2: Then you hear a voice inside you telling you to get up and try again.

Player 4: That's when you've heard the voice of courage.

(Unison action. This can be a group "high five," for example. It must be a childish action and bring a giggle to the audience as well as the actors involved. Saying in unison, "Found courage! Found courage!" in a rap while striking a pose is another method that will bring a laugh.)

Player 2: Oh! I think I know where to find courage!

Player 3: Where?

(Group begins to form a baseball scene with a pitcher, a catcher, and a batter.)

Player 2: When you get up to bat,

(Pitcher tosses an imaginary ball to Player 2 [batter], who strikes and misses.)

Player 2: and strike out,

(Pitches keep coming, Player 2 continues to strike and miss.)

Player 2: and strike out,

Player 4: and strike out.

(The action breaks and the group moves to console Player 2.)

Player 5: The game is over and you go home and want to quit,

Player 1: but you hear a voice telling you not to give up....

Player 2: So you decide to try one more time.

Player 5: That's courage.

(Unison action.)

Player 3: I know where I've seen courage.

(Group forms a group of bullies harassing one child.)

Player 3: Courage is telling a big bully not to tease your little brother.

(Big brother/sister rescues child.)

Players: *(those not involved in the pantomime turn to the audience and say)* That takes courage!

(Unison action.)

Player 2: I know where to see courage in action!

(Group forms a landing pad with Player 2 as the diver.)

Player 4: Practicing a dive off the diving board.

(The "dive" can be a forward somersault with the cast forming two lines of cheerleaders encouraging diver.)

Player 5: Even though you didn't do it very well the first time,

(diver lands safely)

Player 1: that's courage.

Player 2: Courage is doing something until you get it right.

(Unison action, then four Players break into two groups.)

Player 5: *(speaking as a narrator, looks at first pair in pantomime)* Courage is talking things over with Dad when you've done something wrong.

Player 5: *(looks at second pair)* Courage is saying, "I'm sorry," when you fight with your best friend.

(Unison action.)

Player 1: I know where to see an example of courage.

(Players 1, 2, and 5 become test-takers, with cheaters behind them)

Player 3: Where?

Player 1: When a friend wants to copy your paper,

Player 5: or see the answers on the test,

Player 2: courage is saying,

Players 1, 2, 5: "No!"

(Unison action.)

Player 3: I think courage means to stand firm.

(Group forms a line of stiff soldiers.)

All: Stand firm?

Player 2: Like toy soldiers?

Player 1: *(walks stiffly and salutes)* What's brave about standing still?

(Group forms a human "safety net" behind Player 1.)

Player 3: Fall back.

Player 1: Huh?

Player 3: Stand still and fall backward. We'll catch you.

Player 1: How do I know you'll catch me?

All: Trust us.

Player 1: I'm scared!

Player 3: Trust us. Stand firm and then relax in the faith that we will take care of you.

Player 1: I don't know about this.

Player 3: We would never let you get hurt. We will protect you. Have faith.

Player 1: Here goes! *(falls backward)*

Player 4: That did take courage!

(Unison action, then group returns to the arm-in-arm childish pose they began with.)

Player 5: And so the friends who went in search of courage, learned where to find it.

(Group begins to snake their arms, pausing with each line.)

Player 4: Sometimes courage is a voice telling your heart to be brave.

Player 2: Sometimes courage is acting brave even though you are scared.

Player 3: Sometimes courage means you have to trust someone else.

Player 5: Sometimes courage takes faith.

Player 1: Stand strong and be courageous. God is watching out for you.

Every Knee Shall Bow
Praising God In Song

Theme

    This is a readers' theater based on Revelation 5-6.

Cast

    Four voices, male or female — Voice 1 must sing a solo

Staging

    Each person stands holding a folder. There are moments when the whole group sings. Phrases of songs are sung as a backdrop to the dialogue and are not intended to be "solo" moments.

———

Voice 1: *(sings this line and fades as the dialogue begins)* Lead me gently home, Father, lead me gently home.[1]

Voice 2: Imagine going directly into heaven, through the open door. Imagine approaching God.

All: *(whispering)* God,

Voice 4: who created you out of nothing.

Voice 3: God, who formed your eyes so you can see,

Voice 1: who formed your ears so you can hear,

Voice 4: who formed your heart so you can live,

Voice 2: who knit together your DNA structure in your mother's womb,

Voices 3 and 4: and who called you into existence.

All: The God who is and who always has been and always will be.

Voice 2: What would it be like to approach God

Voice 1: who created not only the thousands of stars we see in the nighttime sky,

Voices 1 and 2: but billions and billions of galaxies strewn across the vast universe,

Voices 3 and 4: held together by his purposeful hand and fit together in perfect order?

All: God is everything, and we are nothing.

Voice 1: I can only imagine.

Voice 2: I can only imagine.

Voice 3: I can only imagine.

Voice 4: There in my Father's home, safe and at rest, there in my Savior's love.

Voice 1: Approaching God, we are filled with an overwhelming dread, a sense of mystery, and awe.

Voice 2: O Lord, my God! How great art thou!

Voice 3: When our faith will become sight.

All: *(sing)* There is a place of quiet rest,
near to the heart of God;
A place where sin cannot molest,
near to the heart of God.[2]

Voice 1: We are the created,

All: he is the Creator.

Voice 2: As we approach, our senses have never before experienced such overwhelming power and awesomeness.

Voice 3: Our ears are deadened by the loud thunder emanating from his throne,

Voice 4: our eyes are blinded by the lightning and brightness all around him,

Voice 1: our minds are at once stimulated more than they ever have been and numbed by the awesome realization of God's greatness.

All: *(in whispered awe)* God is so much more, more in every way, than we had imagined.

Voice 2: Everything in us wants to back away from the danger.

Voice 3: And yet,

Voice 4: and yet,

Voices 1 and 2: we can't make ourselves move.

Voice 3: *(speaks softly)* Surrounded by your glory, what would I feel?

Voice 4: We're terrified, to be sure, but there's more delight in the terror than we've ever before experienced.

Voice 1: *(sings softly)* Praise the God of our salvation;
Hosts on high, his power proclaim.
Heaven and earth and all creation,
Laud and magnify his name.[3]

Voice 2: Not able to go forward toward the throne because of fear, but also not able to move away because of joy, we do the only thing we can do, we fall on our faces in awe.

Voice 4: We lie prostrate, warmed by his light and the thought that here is the source,

Voice 2: but shocked by his sheer awesomeness and our own minute smallness.

Voice 3: We look around,

Voice 1: and for the first time,

Voice 4: we notice that we are not alone in worshiping God.

All: All of creation is singing in unison, praise to the one on the throne.

Voice 2: We at last realize that all that is beautiful and best,

Voices 1 and 2: all that is right and true, are from him.

Voice 3: All the complexity and beauty of nature,

Voice 4: all the creatures that creep on the earth,

Voice 2: the animals and plants in all their variety,

Voice 1: the many-colored flowers, deep blue seas,

Voice 3: majestic snow-capped peaks, the grandeur of canyons,

Voice 4: the vast variety and complexity of life,

Voice 1: all reflect

All: the glory of God.

Voices 2 and 4: Suddenly,

Voice 3: we realize there is nothing outside his control, there is nothing in this creation that cannot offer him acceptable praise,

Voice 4: and that all things indeed reach up to glorify him and relish in his glory.

Voice 1: As we are caught up in this praise, we shout aloud,

Voice 2: we laugh,

Voice 4: we raise our hands,

Voice 3: we *(pause)* bow low,

Voice 1: we give all we have to him

All: who was, who is, who is to come! We worship!

Voice 2: God himself has offered the sacrifice, and his Son is it!

Voice 4: As tears stream from our eyes, realizing this awesome sacrifice and that there is nothing we can give in return, we lie prostrate again.

Voice 3: We join with thousands upon thousands of others in communal song,

Voice 2: singing the new song.

Voice 1: We sing to the God who makes all things new,

Voice 4: who is forever dynamic in our lives,

Voice 2: and whose praises never grow tired or dull.

Voice 3: All humankind joins in the assembly,

Voices 1, 2, and 3: and there are no longer any divisions,

All: for we are all one in Jesus Christ. *(pause)*
All hail the power of Jesus' name!
Let angels prostrate fall;
Bring forth the royal diadem,
and crown him Lord of all.[4]

---

1. "Lead Me Gently Home, Father" by Will L. Thompson, 1879, in the public domain.

2. "Near To The Heart Of God" by Cleland B. McAfee, 1903, in the public domain.

3. "Praise The Lord, Ye Heavens Adore Him" by John H. Wilcox, 1797, in the public domain.

4. "All Hail The Power Of Jesus' Name" by Edward Perronet, 1779, in the public domain.

The Joy We Share
The Amazing Power Of The Holy Spirit

Theme

This is a readers' theater written for women.

Cast

Four female voices — Voices 1 and 2 sing duets

Staging

All stand facing the audience. They may have the scripts in their folders.

Note: The scripture references should not be spoken; they are for notation purposes only.

———————

Voices 1 and 2: *(singing duet)* And he walks with me, and he talks with me, and he tells me I am his own, and the joy we share as we tarry there, none other has ever known.[1]

Voice 3: Look at her. Her life is filled with sorrow, yet she remains calm, at peace, and joyful.

Voice 4: How does that happen?

Voice 1: Look at her. Her husband has been unemployed for months, yet she is smiling and trusting.

Voice 4: How does that happen?

Voice 2: Look at her. She is facing serious health issues, and yet she brings laughter to us.

Voice 4: How does that happen?

Voice 3: She walks with the Lord.

Voice 4: *(echoes with a whisper)* She walks with the Lord.

Voices 1 and 2: *(singing duet)* I come to the garden alone, while the dew is still on the roses, and the voice I hear falling on my ear, the Son of God discloses.

Voice 3: May the God of hope fill you with all joy and peace as you trust in him

Voice 4: so that you may overflow with hope by the power of the Holy Spirit (Romans 15:13).

Voice 1: The God of hope. It happens because he gives us hope.

Voice 2: He fills us with joy and peace. It happens because he fills us with joy and peace.

Voice 4: Can it happen for me?

Voice 3: Trust in him so that you may overflow with hope by the power of the Holy Spirit (Romans 15:14).

Voice 1: It happens through trust.

Voice 2: *(sings solo)* When we walk with the Lord, in the light of his word, what a glory he sheds on our way.

Voice 1: *(sings, adding her voice to Voice 2)* While we do his good will, he abides with us still, and with all....[2]

All: *(spoken in unison)* and with *everyone* who will *(pause)* trust and obey.

Voice 3: Look at her, she has no joy. She does not know peace.

Voice 2: She is burdened. She is filled with despair.

Voice 4: Why has that happened?

Voice 1: She doesn't know he can be trusted.

Voice 3: The Lord is my strength and my shield; my heart trusts in him, and I am helped (Psalm 28:7).

Voice 2: When anxiety was great within me, your consolation brought joy to my soul (Psalm 90:14).

Voice 4: She hasn't found his peace. O Lord,

Voice 3: let all who take refuge in you be glad; let them ever sing for joy. Spread your protection over them, that those who love your name may rejoice in you (Psalm 5:11).

Voice 4: This is our prayer.

Voice 1: She hasn't found the amazing power of his Holy Spirit. The scriptures promise:

Voice 2: The Lord has done great things for us and we are filled with joy (Psalm 126:3).

Voice 3: He will fill your mouth with laughter and your lips with shouts of joy (Job 8:21).

Voice 4: He fills your hearts with joy (Acts 14:17).

All: Trust and obey.

Voice 3: We want the laughter. We want the joy.

Voice 4: What does he want us to do? How do I receive this beautiful gift?

Voices 1 and 2: Shout with joy, all the earth! Sing the glory of his name;

Voices 3 and 4: make his praise glorious! Say to God,

All: "How awesome are your deeds!" (Psalm 66:1).

Voice 2: Be joyful always,

Voice 1: pray continually,

Voice 4: give thanks in all circumstances.

Voices 2 and 3: For this is God's will for you in Jesus Christ (1 Thessalonians 5:16).

Voice 1: May our cry be that of the psalmist:

Voice 4: Restore to me the joy of your salvation and grant me a willing spirit to sustain me (Psalm 51:12).

Voices 1 and 2: *(singing duet)* I come to the garden alone, while the dew is still on the roses, and the voice I hear falling on my ear, the Son of God discloses....

Voice 3: Welcome the message with the joy given by the Holy Spirit (1 Thessalonians 1:6).

(The following should cascade on top of each other rapidly.)

Voice 4: He is worthy.

Voice 1: He is mighty.

Voice 2: He is our strength.

Voice 3: He is our refuge.

Voice 4: He can be trusted.

Voices 1 and 2: He is sovereign.

All: He is King of kings and Lord of Lords.

Voice 4: Sing for joy to God our strength (Psalm 81:1).

Voice 3: Tell of his works with songs of joy (Psalm 107:22).

Voice 2: Satisfy us in the morning with your unfailing love,

Voice 1: that we may sing for joy and be glad all our days.

All: Clap your hands, all you nations; shout to God with cries of joy.

Voices 3 and 4: How awesome is the Lord most high, the great king over all the earth (Psalm 47:1).

Voices 1 and 2: *(singing duet)* And he walks with me and he talks with me, and he tells me I am his own, and the joy we share as we tarry there, none other has ever known.

Voice 3: Look at her, she knows the Lord.

Voice 4: Look at her, she is filled with joy.

Voice 1: Look at her,

Voice 2: through her ... we see joy in him.

All: *(reverently)* May he fill your hearts with joy.

---

1. "In The Garden" by Austin Miles, 1913, in the public domain.

2. "Trust And Obey" by John H. Sammis, 1887, in the public domain.

Who Is In Control?
A Look At The Apostle Paul's Mother

Theme

This monologue takes a look at choices a grown child makes and the impact it has on his parents.

Cast

    Narrator (female)

    Saul's Mother

Staging

This fictional account is spoken by a woman portraying Saul's mother. The tone begins with one of pride, but changes as she recalls events to include anger, fear, confusion, conviction, and ultimately reluctant acceptance that it is God who is really in control. A scroll is needed, halfway through the monologue.

———

Narrator: As a young mother, I controlled my children's movements. I controlled what they ate, where they slept, where they went to school, and even to some degree, who their friends were. As they grew, I allowed them to make some of their own decisions, still monitoring their choices very carefully. Every mother of a teenager will recognize the "near panic feeling" that occurs when your child makes decisions that are completely beyond your control. Our intentions are noble. We want to protect them. We want to guide them and keep them from making simple mistakes. We want to instill godly values and watch them grow into fine Christian young people.

Many women find it bewildering when their children choose paths very different from what they had envisioned. We all reach that moment when we must let go and trust in God's provision. We discover that we are not the ones in control.

Let me tell you about a biblical character, the apostle Paul. This man was truly passionate about his Lord. He was a "Jew of all Jews," meaning that he came from an educated Jewish family and was a devoted practitioner of the faith. Admired by all — he might have had a very proud mother. The scriptures tell us that he was first known as Saul, and he was passionate about persecuting the Christians. God had to strike him with a blinding light on the road to Damascus and tell him that Jesus was indeed the Christ before Saul would believe. It was at the point of conversion that Saul became Paul.

Let's think a few moments about Paul's mother. The scriptures do not tell us what his mother thought about her son's radical conversion. Perhaps she was a mother who was bewildered, disappointed, frustrated, and maybe even angry with her child's choices. Maybe you, too, have felt this way. Let's hear what Saul's mother has to say.

Saul's Mother: I am the mother of a grown son, and I, like all mothers, I suppose, am so proud of him. You see, from early childhood, it was obvious to us that we had a boy with extraordinary faith. Of course, why should we be surprised? After all, genetics do matter, eh? We came from a long line of faithful men and women of God. We could proudly quote the family tree claiming the pillars of the faith as blood ties. His father and I have loved the Lord all our lives. It gave us pure joy to see our child in love with the same God we worship. It isn't just a religion to us. It is a lifestyle. From the cradle, we taught him the truth. We told him about an amazing, loving, awesome God and explained that he was born into a community of believers that were the chosen people of God. My husband spared no expense in securing an excellent education for him. My husband was insistent that his son be trained by the most reputable, knowledgable men available concerning the law.

I suppose I could have been a bragging mother — "Well, you know *my son* got the best grades in his class," ... "Yes, he did get a scholarship to the best university," — but instead I was continually humbled by his passion and sincere, earnest desire to do the Lord's will. Who was I to boast? God was doing wonderful work in a man who happened to live under my roof. I was honored.

I am still honored, but I'm not at all happy with the Lord right now.

It all began with his conversion to Christianity. You see, we had all been appalled at the number of people who were saying the Messiah had come and had been crucified. As if God, Lord of heaven and earth, would allow such a thing! We were, it is true, all waiting and watching for the prophesied Messiah, but when he came, it would certainly not be as a criminal. That seemed absurd. We found the idea highly offensive. To discover that Saul was actively attempting to stifle this blasphemy did not surprise us; as a matter of fact, we appreciated his stand for the Lord Almighty. These people had to be stopped.

My life changed forever the day my son came home from Damascus. He, along with his companions, told us an unbelievable story of a miraculous revelation from Christ himself on the road to Damascus. He claimed the true Messiah had come to him in a blinding light on the road and instructed him to seek out a certain man who would explain the truth to him. Saul told the events of the following days and concluded with the announcement that he was now a believer. Not only that, but his name was forever changed to Paul.

I heard his story, I saw the same passion and love for the Lord that had always been a part of him. Now, however, it was pointed in a different direction. Did I believe him? *(conflicted and hesitantly)* Yes. Could I believe that the Lord would talk to my son and give him a special assignment here on earth? Yes. Not surprising to me. Did I believe that Jesus was indeed the Messiah? *(pauses and the struggle in her face unfolds as she resolves this issue)* Yes. After hearing the story, yes.

After a couple days of questions and answers ... after the shock had worn off, I became angry. This sounds so petty. After all, who am I to argue with the Lord? But Saul was cutting himself off from his heritage of faith, his family tree, our entire community of friends and associates, and not only that, *he was even changing his name!* The name his father and I gave him. The name that had a special place in my heart. Oh, it didn't bother him. He had a mission. He had a purpose. He was on fire for the Lord. He had been given this new name by Christ.

So who was I? Not someone who had any control over the situation. I had to accept the will of the Lord. But I could see the other ramifications. A quiet voice in the back of my mind said, "But what about me?"

(as if she is one of the local gossips) "Oh, there is Saul's mother. Poor thing. Did you hear he went insane and is now preaching that Jesus is Christ? He even changed his name. He thinks God gave it to him. They must be so embarrassed, and he had such a promising career ahead of him. How could they possibly let their son make a fool of himself? Don't they know the story of Eli? We are obviously looking at another bad father. He should discipline his own son."

(directed at God) God? Could you just strike all my friends and family with blinding light and tell them that my precious son is really doing your will? They think he's a lunatic. *(pauses)* While you are at it, I haven't heard from you, either. How am I supposed to defend my son? A little voice telling me what to do would be nice. *(pauses)*

It was not hard to believe the gospel when we were in the presence of Paul. He had an authority about him that made you confident he spoke the truth. I could still look at him and be proud to be his mother. I was proud to know that he was doing important work for the Lord.

We had only begun adjusting to the stigma involved as the parents of an apostle, living in a Jewish community when we got the next blow.

(unrolls scroll and reads) Hi, Mom. What's new? I'm fine, thank you. I thought I would let you know that God has given me a new assignment. He gave me a dream that explained it to me. God is sending me to preach to the Gentiles. *(extremely frustrated)* Why me, Lord? *(rolls up scroll)*

(to herself) Let's review.

1. Do I believe Jesus is the Messiah? Yes.
2. Do I believe the Jews must accept him for salvation? Yes.
3. Do I believe the Jews are the chosen people of God? Yes.

40

4. Do I believe that God can do anything he wants to, that if he wants to allow Gentiles to have salvation, that it's not my business? Yes.

But *why* does it have to be my son that converts them? I'm really never going to be able to show my face at the local quilting club again. Doesn't Paul realize what bridges he's burning with his own family tree? What do I tell them at the next family reunion? These are family members that love Paul — are concerned for his spiritual welfare. They fear for his eternal life. He might as well have leprosy.

It's easy to say that you shouldn't care about what people think, especially if you know it's God's will. But, what if those people are good and faithful men and women who have served the Lord for generations? They truly believe that our son has "left the faith." I thought I could help a little by suggesting that if these people wanted to be Christians, they could at least be circumcised and learn to eat kosher foods ... just to fit in better with the community. Well, he set me straight on that one. He's throwing out several hundred years of tradition, insisting that the Gentiles don't have to be bound by the law. Christ came to fulfill the law. *(reluctantly nods in acquiescence)*

It's still going to be really hard to take his new friends to the church potluck.

Do I sound shallow and trivial? Perhaps I am. All mothers want their children to be happy and successful, well-received by their peers. In my marriage, our goal was to develop God-fearing, God-loving, God-serving children. That happened — just not in the manner we envisioned. What did that cost Paul? The loss of family ties, loss of a prestigious career, loss of respect in our religious community, loss of friendships, and perhaps, even someday ... loss of his very life for Christ's sake — an enormous price. But, he "counts it all worthless to gain Christ Jesus."

The cost for me? *(humorously)* No one in the synagogue ever asked my husband and I to teach a workshop on raising children in the faith. Real sacrifices? Nothing in comparison to the blessings showered on me. God gave me an amazing blessing through my son. He brought me to the knowledge of Christ Jesus and what it means to have freedom in him. I'm proud to be Christ's child and Paul's mother.

www.ingramcontent.com/pod-product-compliance
Lightning Source LLC
Chambersburg PA
CBHW071105040426
42443CB00008B/965